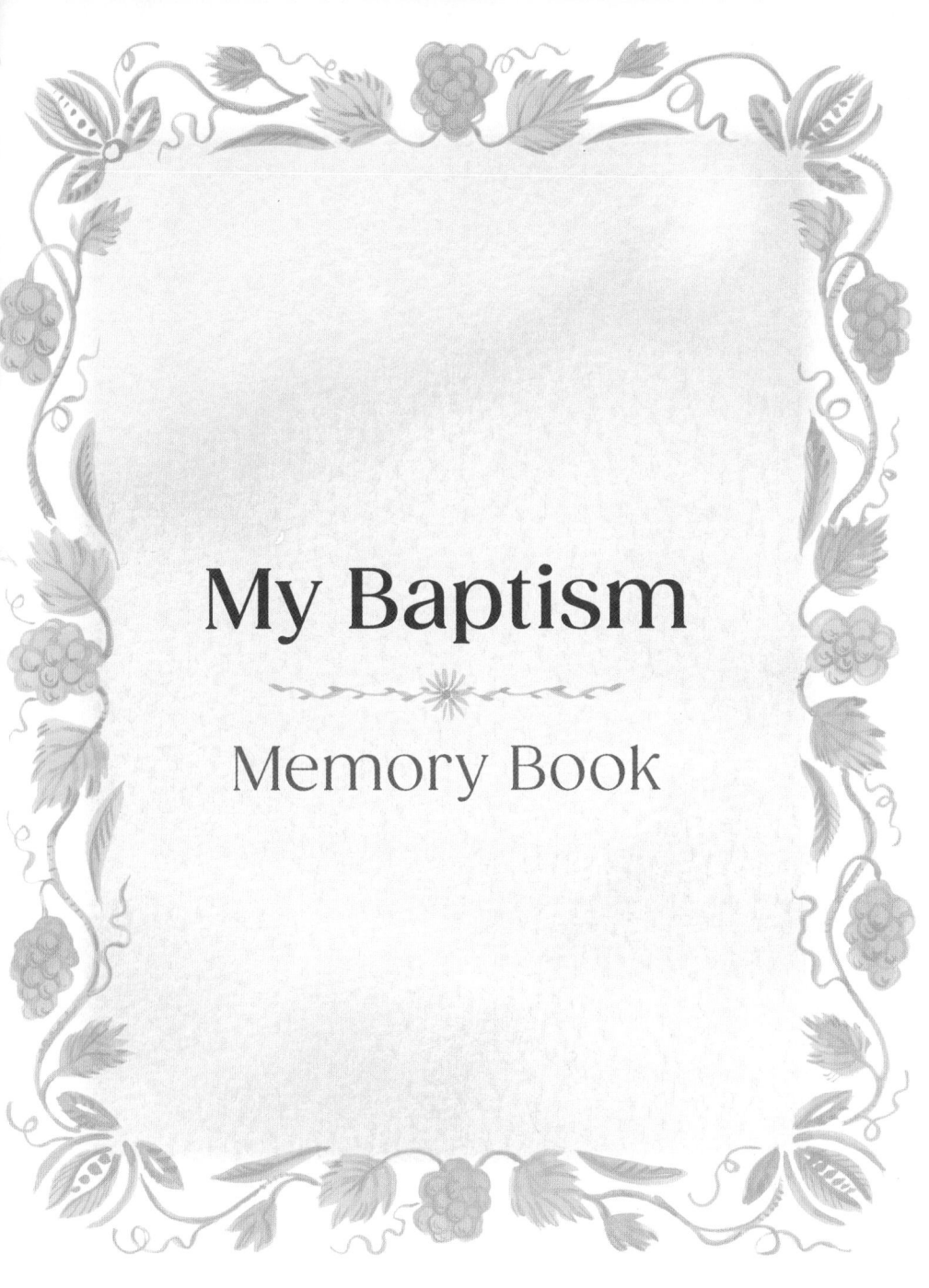

My Baptism

Memory Book

Place your photo here

All About Me

Full name

Date of birth

Place of birth

Parents' names

Godparents' names

My name means

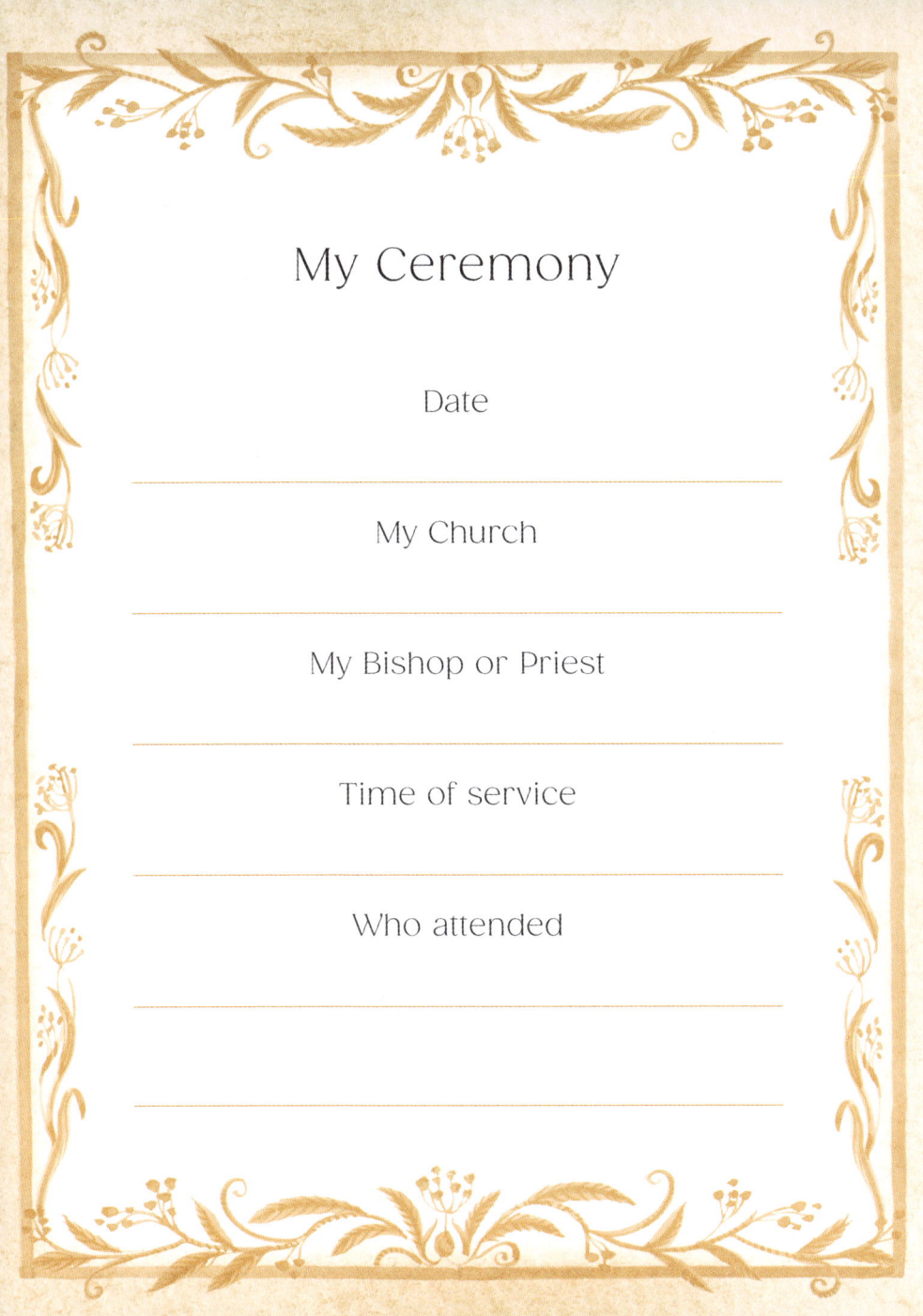

My Ceremony

Date

My Church

My Bishop or Priest

Time of service

Who attended

"Therefore if anyone is in Christ, he is a new creation.

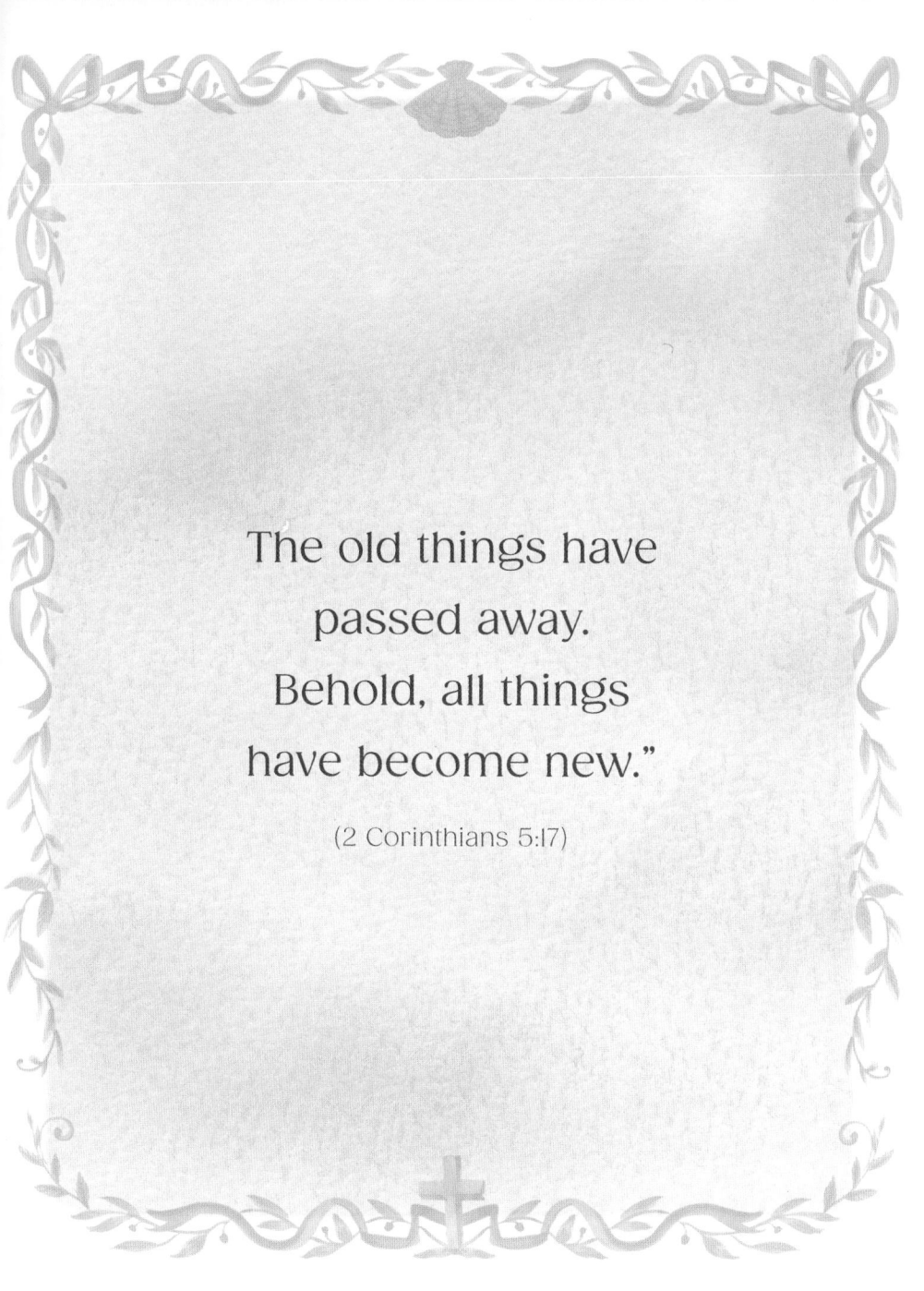

The old things have passed away. Behold, all things have become new."

(2 Corinthians 5:17)

What is Baptism?

Baptism welcomes someone into the family of God. It is the start of a new life in Jesus Christ. In baptism, we use water as a symbol of washing away the old and getting ready for the new.

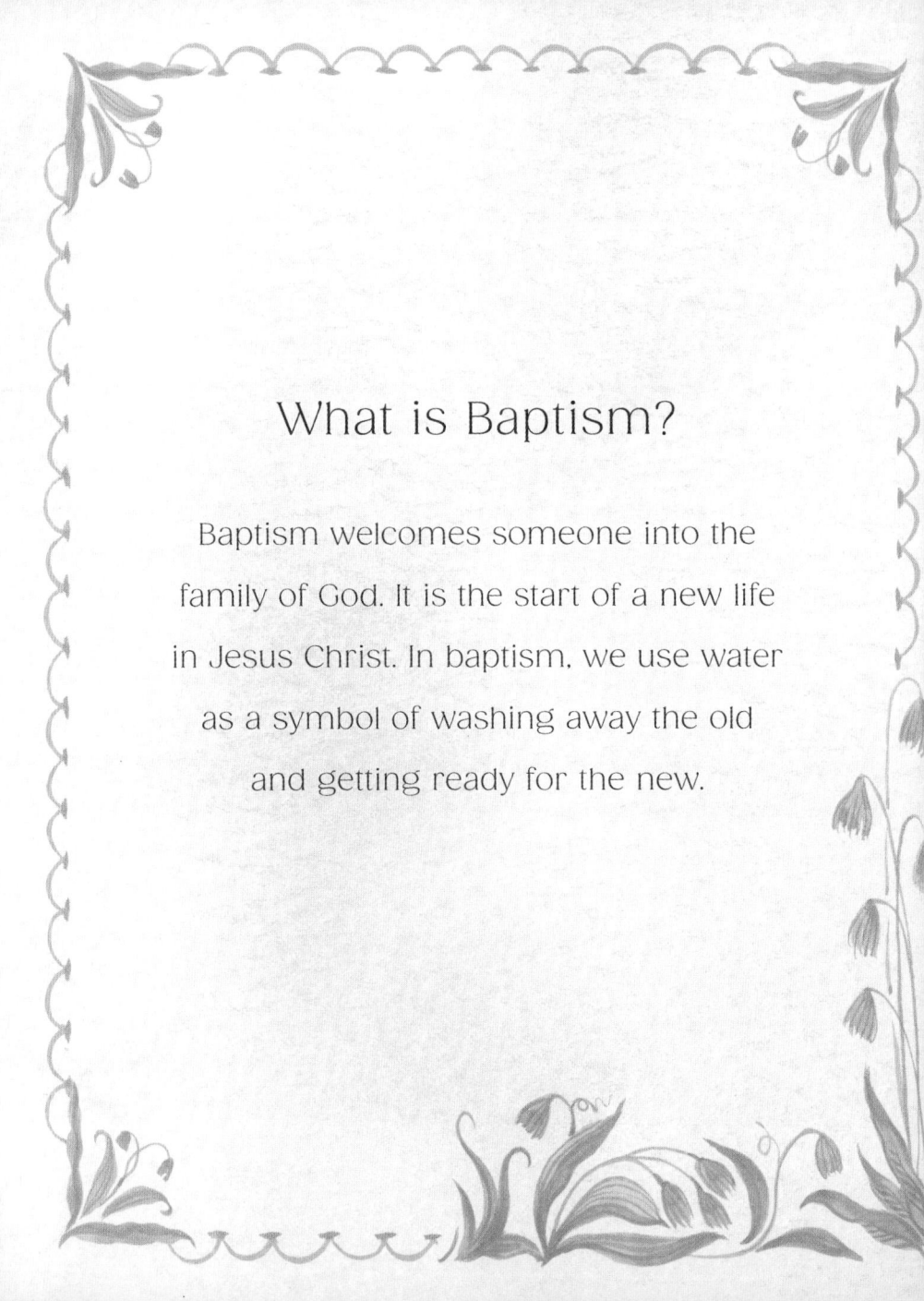

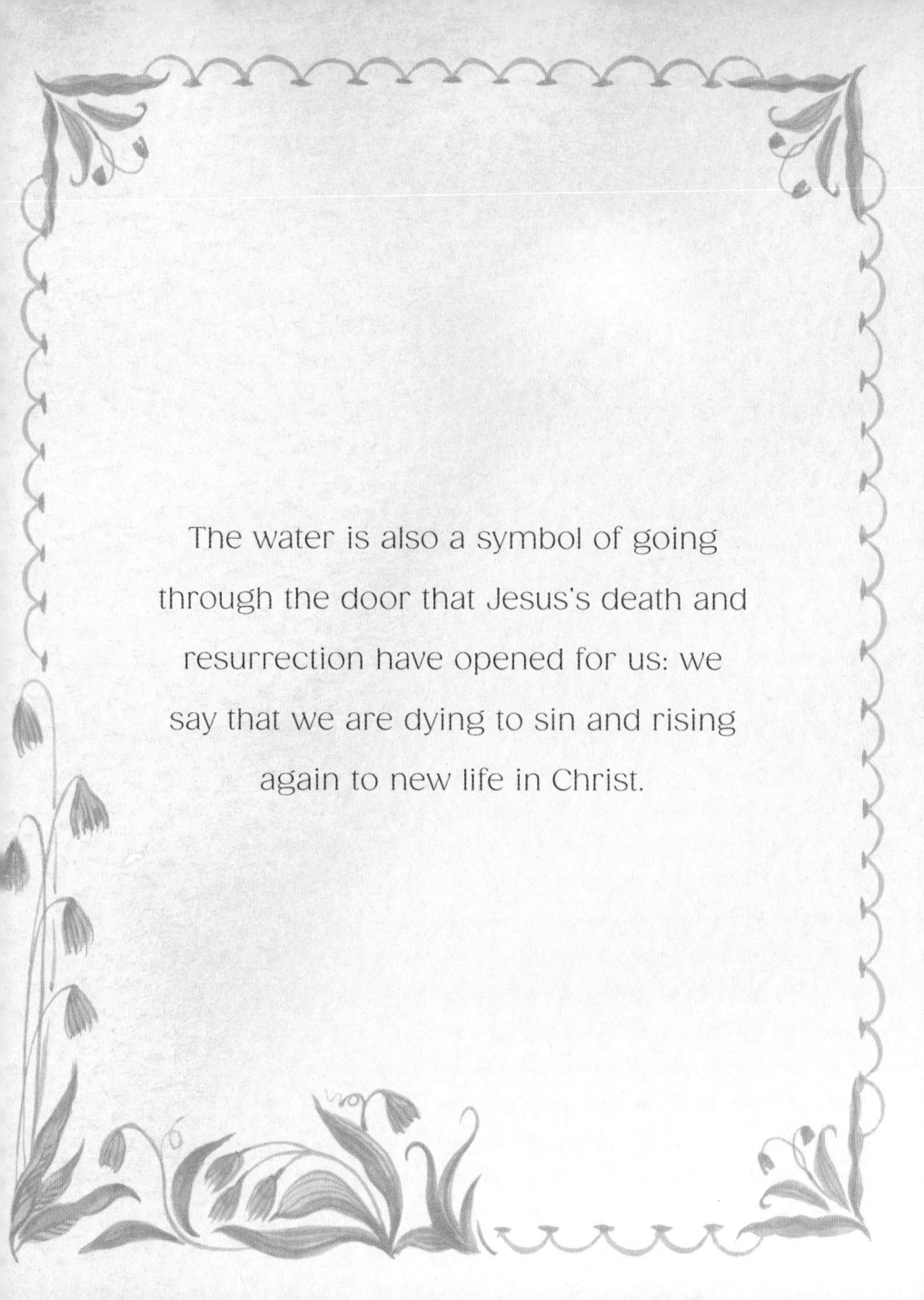

The water is also a symbol of going through the door that Jesus's death and resurrection have opened for us: we say that we are dying to sin and rising again to new life in Christ.

My Ceremony

Place your photo here

Place your photo here

"'Repent and be baptized, every one of you, in the name of Jesus Christ for the forgiveness of sins, and you will receive the gift of the Holy Spirit.

For the promise is to you and to your children, and to all who are far off, even as many as the Lord our God will call to himself.'"

(Acts 2:38-39)

Our Traditions

How our family celebrates special occasions

_____

_____

_____

How our family celebrates Easter

_____

_____

_____

How our family
celebrates Christmas

Our family traditions

Symbols of Baptism

There are many different symbols associated with this special day. Which ones did we see?

Water
Symbolising being
cleaned from sin

A scallop shell
Symbolising the start of
your journey of faith

Oil
Symbolising that
it is now harder for evil
to grasp on to you

A candle
Symbolising your
enlightenment and the light
you shine in the world

The sign of the cross
Symbolising Jesus's death
giving new life

White clothes
Symbolising
a fresh start

Memorable Moments

The weather on the day of my Baptism

Family traditions we honoured

My mood

My Church

Place your photo here

Place your photo here

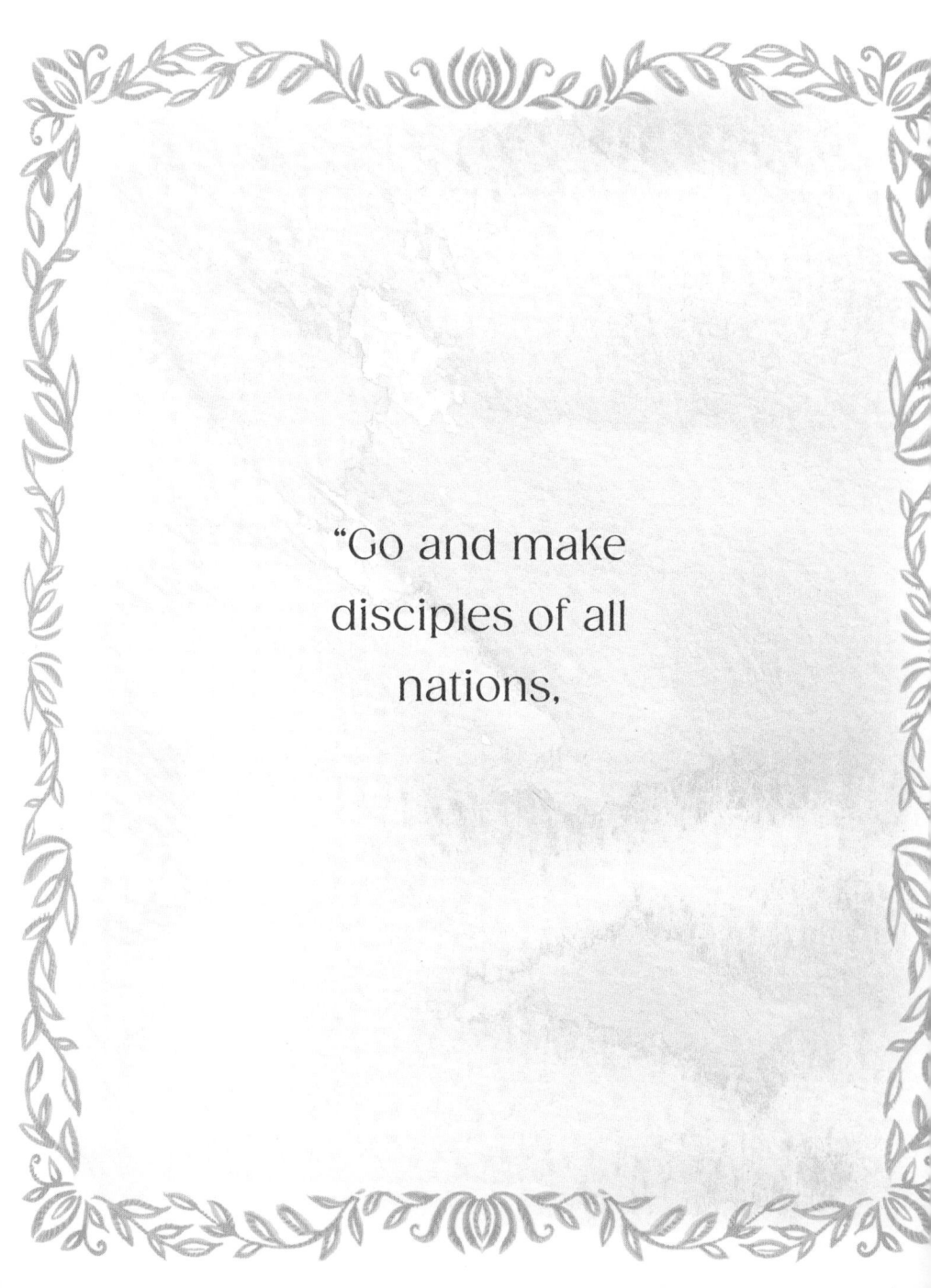

"Go and make disciples of all nations,

baptizing them in
the name of the
Father and of the
Son and of the
Holy Spirit,"

(Matthew 28:19)

Promises made to me today

Promises I made today

The Sign of the Cross

"In the name

of the Father,

and of the Son,

and of the Holy Spirit.

Amen."

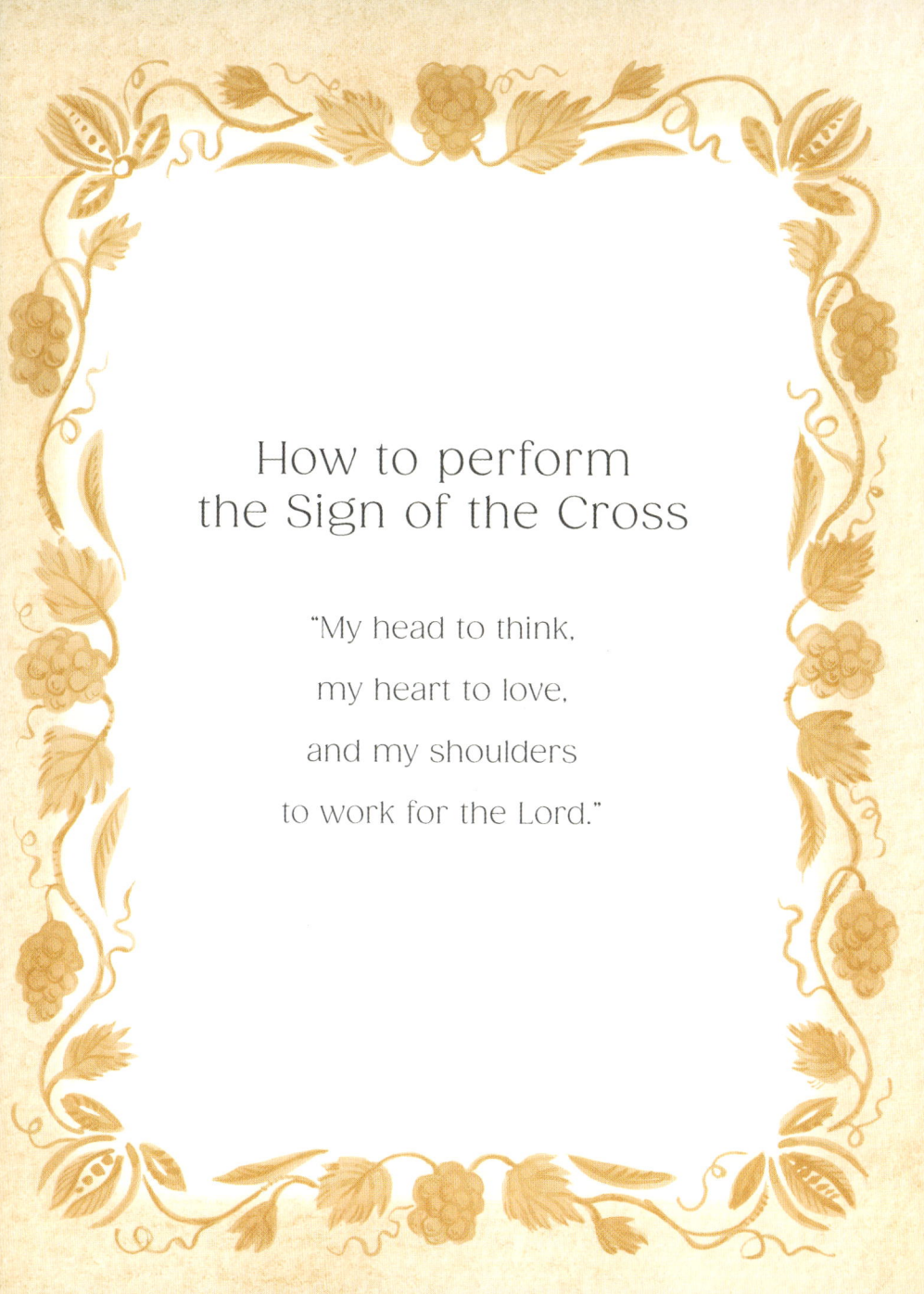

How to perform the Sign of the Cross

"My head to think,

my heart to love,

and my shoulders

to work for the Lord."

Hymns that we sang

The Story of Noah's Ark

People didn't love God like he wanted, and were not treating each other nicely. So God decided to flood the world. He warned a good man, called Noah.

Noah listened to God. He built a big boat, called an ark. Then he led pairs of each animal into the ark and climbed aboard with his family.

Then the rain came. It rained for 40 days and 40 nights. The entire Earth was flooded, but everything on the boat was safe. Then the rain stopped.

Noah sent out a dove. When it came back with a leaf, he knew the flood was over. God promised never to flood the whole world again. He put a beautiful rainbow in the sky to remind us of his promise.

Gifts given to me on my special day

Finding love and happiness

"God is love, and he who remains in love remains in God, and God remains in him. In this, love has been made perfect among us, that we may have boldness in the day of judgment, because as he is, even so we are in this world.

There is no fear in love;
but perfect love casts out
fear, because fear has
punishment. He who fears is
not made perfect in love. We
love him, because he
first loved us."

(1 John 4:16-19)

"Jesus answered, 'Most certainly I tell you,

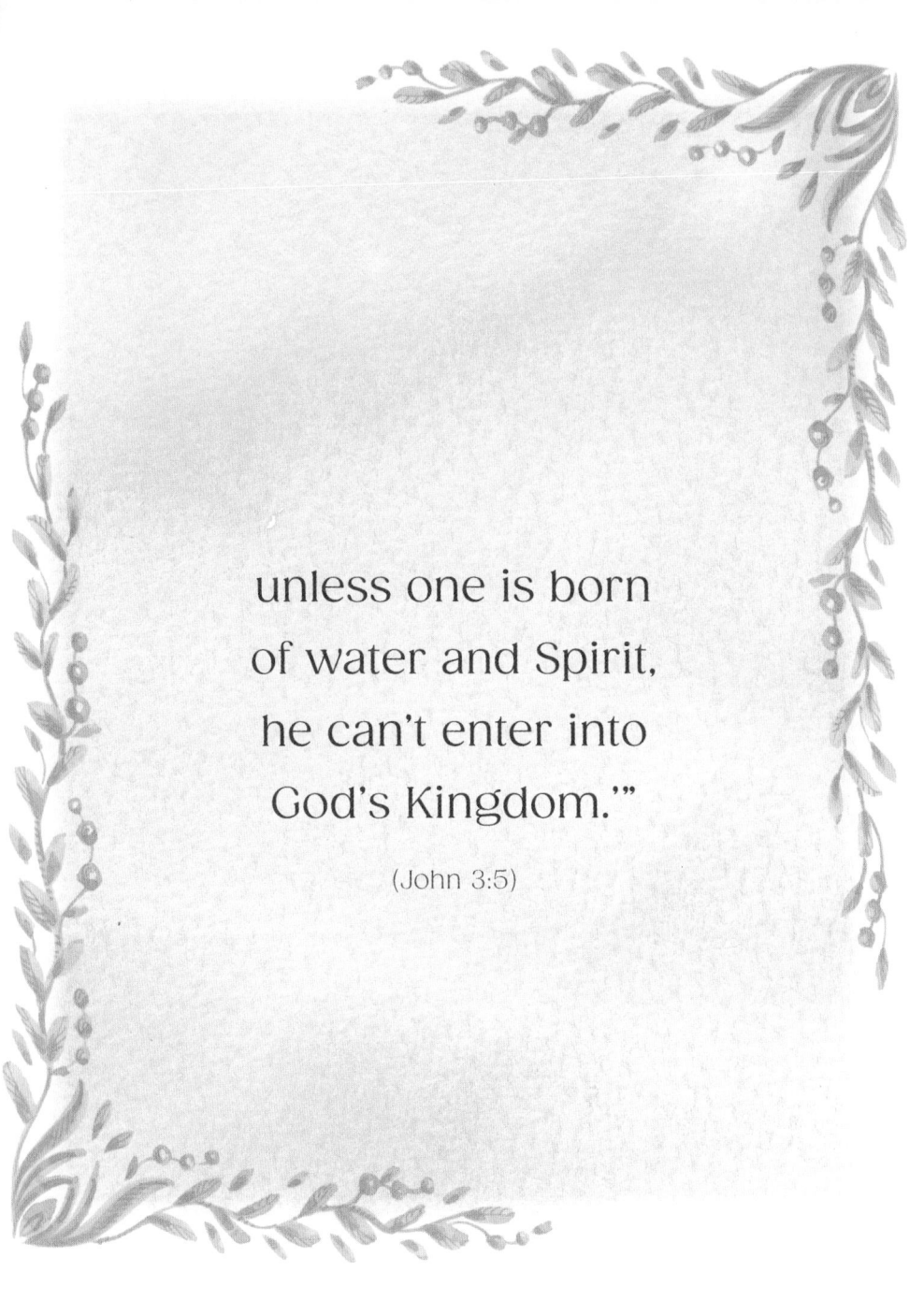

unless one is born
of water and Spirit,
he can't enter into
God's Kingdom.'"

(John 3:5)

Just as I am
by Charlotte Elliott

Just as I am, without one plea,
but that thy blood was shed for me,
and that thou bidd'st me come
to thee, O Lamb of God,
I come, I come.

Just as I am, and waiting not
to rid my soul of one dark blot,
to thee, whose blood can cleanse
each spot, O Lamb of God,
I come, I come.

Just as I am, though tossed about
with many a conflict, many a doubt,
fightings and fears within, without,
O Lamb of God,
I come, I come.

Just as I am, thou wilt receive,
wilt welcome, pardon, cleanse,
relieve; because thy promise
I believe, O Lamb of God,
I come, I come.

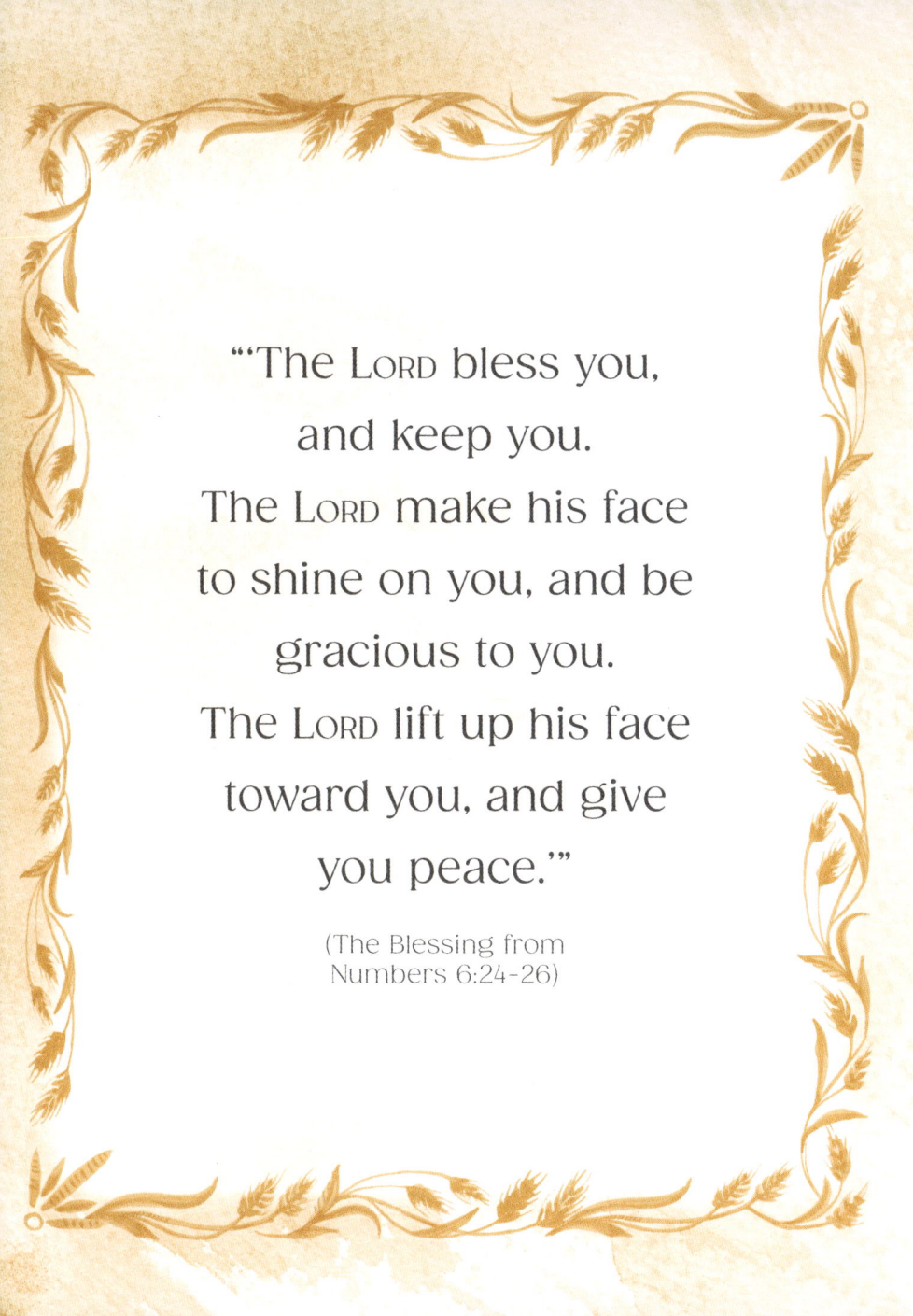

"'The Lord bless you, and keep you. The Lord make his face to shine on you, and be gracious to you. The Lord lift up his face toward you, and give you peace.'"

(The Blessing from Numbers 6:24-26)

"'This is my
beloved Son,

with whom I am
well pleased.'"

(Matthew 3:17)

A letter for the future

A letter for the future

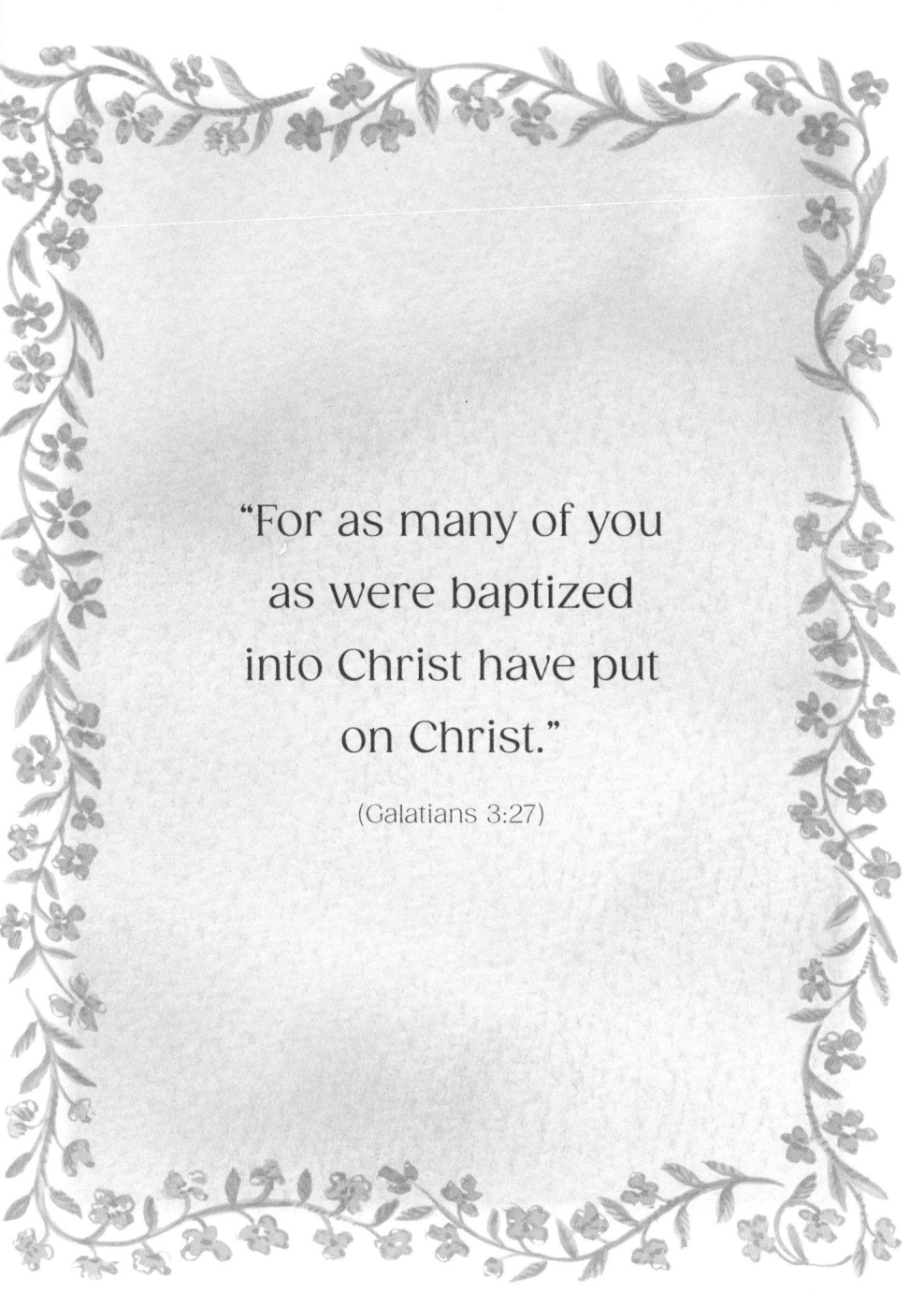

"For as many of you as were baptized into Christ have put on Christ."

(Galatians 3:27)

Thoughts, hopes, and messages

from those who matter most

Thoughts, hopes, and messages

from those who matter most

Thoughts, hopes, and messages

from those who matter most

Thoughts, hopes, and messages

from those who matter most

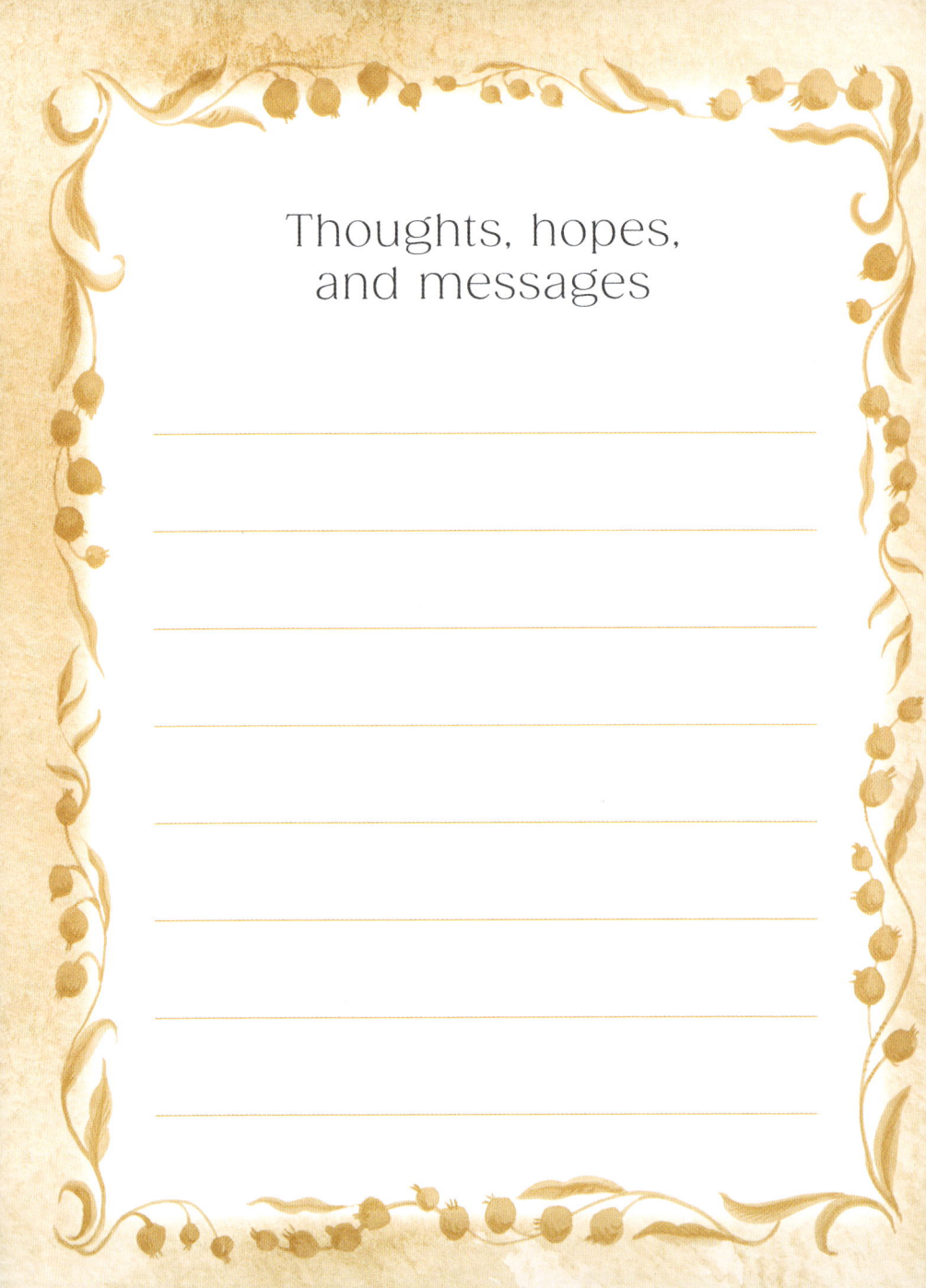

Thoughts, hopes, and messages

from those who matter most

Thoughts, hopes, and messages

from those who matter most

Thoughts, hopes, and messages

from those who matter most

Thoughts, hopes, and messages

from those who matter most

Thoughts, hopes, and messages

from those who matter most

Thoughts, hopes, and messages

from those who matter most

Place your photo here

Place your photo here

Place your photo here

Place your photo here

Place your photo here

Place your photo here

Place your photo here

Place your photo here

Place your photo here

Place your photo here

Place your photo here

Place your photo here

Place your photo here

Place your photo here

Place your photo here

Place your photo here

Place your photo here

Illustrated by Victoria Nelson

First published in Great Britain in 2026 by
Dorling Kindersley Limited
20 Vauxhall Bridge Road,
London SW1V 2SA

The authorised representative in the EEA is
Dorling Kindersley Verlag GmbH. Arnulfstr. 124,
80636 Munich, Germany

Copyright © 2026 Dorling Kindersley Limited
A Penguin Random House Company
10 9 8 7 6 5 4 3 2 1
001-352580-Mar/2026

All Scripture quotations are taken from
the World English Bible (WEB)

All rights reserved.
No part of this publication may be reproduced, stored
in or introduced into a retrieval system, or transmitted,
in any form, or by any means (electronic, mechanical,
photocopying, recording, or otherwise), without the
prior written permission of the copyright owner.
No part of this publication may be used or reproduced in
any manner for the purpose of training artificial intelligence
technologies or systems. In accordance with Article 4(3)
of the DSM Directive 2019/790, DK expressly reserves
this work from the text and data mining exception.

A CIP catalogue record for this book
is available from the British Library.
ISBN: 978-0-2417-7108-2

Printed and bound in India

www.dk.com

This book was made with Forest Stewardship Council™ certified paper – one small step in DK's commitment to a sustainable future. **Learn more at www.dk.com/uk/information/sustainability**